Twenty-five Not Out

A Play

Hazel Wyld

A Samuel French Acting Edition

SAMUEL FRENCH

FOUNDED 1830

SAMUELFRENCH-LONDON.CO.UK
SAMUELFRENCH.COM

CHARACTERS

Diane Blott
Harold Blott
Carole Blott
Bess Johnson
Ben Johnson

The action of the play takes place in the bedroom of the
Blotts' house in the suburbs of London.

Time—the present.

To Roy who isn't a bit like Harold

SCENE 1

The bedroom of a middle-class house somewhere in the suburbs of London. Early Saturday evening

It is a comfortably furnished room with a double bed UC. UL *is a door leading into a bathroom; a further door* UR *leads on to the landing.* DR *is a dressing table with a stool,* DL *a chaise-longue. There are two bedside cabinets either side of the bed, one with a telephone. Directly in front of the chaise-longue is a small coffee table. On the dressing table besides the usual toilet items, there is a glass full of gin and tonic*

When the CURTAIN *rises, Diane Blott, an attractive middle-aged woman, is sitting in front of the dressing table. She is in evening dress and is putting on her make-up, and generally attending to her toilet. Her husband Harold enters from the bathroom. He is half-dressed and proceeds to put on his shirt and jacket which are draped over the bedspread*

Diane I really want this party to go well tonight.

Harold (*not really listening*) Mmm.

Diane I don't want us to start off on the wrong foot but if you cut down on your drinking, I could relax and enjoy myself.

Harold You make me sound like an alcoholic.

Diane Well, I know you don't recognize it but I honestly think you're well on the way.

Harold Cheers. (*He lifts his glass from the dressing table and salutes her*)

Diane This is a special evening you know, not one of your boozy impromptu parties.

Harold I don't have boozy impromptu parties, well, not very often. You have a very chilling effect on any boozy gathering, reeking of disapproval from a corner.

Diane Unfortunately if they are our parties I end up trying to get you to bed before you fall down, and if they are other people's I have to stay stone cold sober all night just in order to drive you home; I would just like our silver wedding celebration to be different, that's all. . . . Do you think I've overdone the eye make-up? (*She looks anxiously at herself in the mirror*)

Harold You look a bit dark round the eyes, I suppose that's the illness.

Diane (*swivelling round to look at him*) What illness?

Harold Your illness.

Diane What are you drivelling on about, I'm not ill.

Harold (*feigning amazement*) You're not ill?

Diane No.

Harold Every night for months you've darted off to bed about ten o'clock and have been sparko when I've come up, naturally I assumed you were ill.

Diane I hold down an important job and I run this house, obviously I get tired but I'm certainly not ill, I just can't keep burning the candle at both ends anymore, we're neither of us getting any younger.

Harold I thought you were ill.

Diane Well I'm not.

Harold You mean to say I've roamed this house night after night searching for tsetse fly and you're not ill.

Diane Very funny.

Harold I'm not looking forward to this do. (*He moves across to look in the dressing table mirror*)

Diane Oh charming!

Harold I'd rather have celebrated our silver wedding quietly, just us and Carole.

Diane It was Carole's idea that we had a party.

Harold I hate parties.

Diane Nonsense you love parties, you're a party person.

Harold Well I hate our parties, I like parties where you can enjoy yourself without the hassle of having to make sure everyone else is having a good time.

Diane That is because basically you are a very selfish person.

Harold (*offended*) Well that's a charming thing to say to your husband on the twenty-fifth anniversay of your wedding-day.

Diane It's the truth. (*She stands up and smooths down her dress*) I knew you were a selfish person before I married you but as I loved you and I was young and foolish I thought I'd be able to change you.

Harold You may have been young but you've never been naïve, behind that fluffy exterior is a mind like a steel trap ... I should know ... I refuse to believe you married me in the belief you would, in the fullness of time, be able to mould me like plasticine ... On second thoughts I take that back, on reflection I expect that was exactly what you thought.

Diane moves upstage and takes out a jewel box from the drawer of the bedside cabinet; she then brings the box down to the dressing table and starts looking through for suitable ear-rings

Diane If I did I was certainly disillusioned fast enough, you've always done exactly as you pleased. I'm just saying ... will you, just for once, drink in moderation?

Harold, still holding his now empty glass, moves upstage and sits on the bed

Harold I always drink in moderation, I do everything in moderation, I am your moderate wage-earner. Every day I trot off to catch the seven forty-five train to the city and every lunchtime I go to the same wine bar for lunch. Then I return home on the six o'clock train, unless I'm entertaining clients; I play golf every Saturday whilst you go shopping for clothes, though why you need to buy clothes every Saturday is totally beyond my comprehension ... In short we lead a totally boring moderate existence which is doubtless why we are giving a totally predictable party for our silver wedding for our equally boring and predictable friends.

Diane sits back down and starts putting on the ear-rings

Diane Oh God, how many did you have at lunchtime?
Harold And that, my dear, is a totally predictable comment.
Diane Harold, I warn you, Carole has gone to a great deal of trouble to arrange this party for us ...
Harold Ah ha ... we've gone from merely suggesting to warning, have we?
Diane I realize you're trying to start a row and I refuse to bite.
Harold I'm not trying to start a row, I just think that pointing out that you consider me half-way to being an alcoholic is not the best way to ensure a pleasant evening.

Diane You deliberately came home late from the golf club, you knew there'd be a million and one things to do . . .

Harold (*playing an imaginary violin*) Carry on . . .

Diane (*getting up and moving over to the bed*) I have no intention of continuing . . . I am going downstairs ready to greet our guests and if you want to get drunk and make a fool of yourself well, bloody well get on with it . . .

She sweeps out, slamming the door behind her

After a short pause, Harold picks up the phone and dials a number

Harold Come on, come on, answer for God's sake . . . (*He shifts the phone to under his chin and looks at his watch*) I suppose they've left already, bloody ridiculous to turn up at eight just because the invite says eight . . . who arrives first at a party . . . (*He slams the phone down and sits despondently on the bed*) This is going to be a fiasco . . . I can feel disaster looming over me.

Diane (*Off*) Harold! Try to hurry, the Johnsons have just pulled up in their car, can you imagine anyone turning up on time?

Harold (*morosely*) Yes.

He exits, re-enters, picks up his glass and gazes into it for a second, then sighs

Happy anniversary!

He exits

Black-out

SCENE 2

The same. Later the same evening

The door opens and Harold enters from the landing. He is carrying a glass and a couple of cans of lager; he also has a newspaper tucked under his arm. He sits down on the chaise-longue, opens a lager and pours himself a drink; he then searches and finds a pen and starts filling in the crossword puzzle

Carole, his daughter, comes in. She is in her early twenties, very pretty and dressed in a short strapless evening dress

Carole I thought this was where you'd be hiding . . . what's up?

Harold Just hiding. (*He doesn't look up*)

Carole What do you mean . . . just hiding . . . this is your party, you can't hide.

Harold (*still apparently engrossed in his paper*) Yes I can . . . I am.

Carole (*crossing over and removing his paper*) Dad, this is your silver-wedding party, everyone here is either a friend of yours or Mum's, who are you hiding from?

Harold I beg to differ, they are not all friends, some of them are family.

Carole sits on the floor next to him and takes a sip from his glass

Carole All right, who's upset you?

Harold (*taking back his newspaper*) No-one's upset me, I felt bored so I came up here to do my crossword and contemplate my navel for a while . . . OK?

Carole You've been acting very strangely all evening.

Harold (*looking shifty*) How?

Carole You're always the life and soul of the party, you drink too much, flirt with all the girls, generally make a fool of yourself . . . you have a great time! Tonight you've skulked about in corners, kept a very low profile and finally sneaked off to sit in the bedroom, now you must admit that's out of character . . . so . . . what's up?

Harold takes his glass from her and refills it from the lager can

Harold Have you ever thought of giving up secretarial work and taking up international espionage?
Carole Don't think I don't know when you're trying to fob me off!
Harold Who's that Kenny Rogers lookalike you've brought with you tonight?
Carole And don't try to change the subject ... anyway how can he be a Kenny Rogers lookalike he's only twenty-three!
Harold Good Lord, is he! (*Looking at his paper*) Try and think of an eleven-letter word meaning "main character in a novel", blank R, blank blank A, last letter T.
Carole All right, I get the message, "Mind your own business ..." I won't ask another question ... (*She looks around*) Do you know I can remember one year you kept sneaking up here in the evenings and it turned out you were making me a doll's house as a surprise for Christmas. Whatever happened to that doll's house? Have you still got it?
Harold I'm saving it for my grandchildren. I suppose I'll have some eventually?
Carole Give me a chance, I've got a lot of living to do.
Harold Why don't you go back to the party? Kenny thingy might have galloped off into the night, shouldn't you be checking up on him instead of me?
Carole His name is Willis and he's much too devoted to me to gallop off anywhere without my giving him permission.
Harold You sound like your mother.
Carole Mother's got as much control over you as a rabbit has over a stoat!
Harold Willis ...? I thought that was tobacco! Not part of a wealthy family, is he?
Carole You're thinking of Wills, actually he's a bank manager's son.
Harold Well I suppose that could be useful ... serious, is it?
Carole (*softly*) Could be.

Diane enters

Diane What on earth are you two doing up here? (*Without waiting for an answer*) Let me guess, one of you is pregnant or the other one is up to something!

Harold (*turning to Carole, taking her hand*) We might as well come clean . . . I'm pregnant!

Diane Very funny.

Carole I just came up here to find Dad.

Harold And I just come up here seeking solitude, which I might add appears to be eluding me.

Diane What on earth are you talking about, this is supposed to be our silver-wedding party.

Harold So it is.

Diane It's a bit of a funny time to be seeking solitude, isn't it?

Harold Yes.

Diane What do you mean "Yes"?

Harold All right . . . No.

Diane (*exasperated*) Harold, I warn you I am not in the mood for one of your silly conversations.

Carole (*rising*) I think I ought to go and find Willis.

Diane You might be too late, the last time I saw him he was being manhandled by that dreadful blonde.

Harold Which dreadful blonde would that be?

Diane You know perfectly well who I mean, your so called friend's wife.

Harold If you mean Ben Johnson I must point out he is a colleague not a friend, also, if I am not mistaken, you invited him and his wife without consulting me.

Diane Is that why you're sulking?

Harold I am not sulking . . . I might be bored but I'm not sulking.

Carole (*moving to the door*) Well, before you get into full swing I'll go and rescue poor Willis.

Diane "Poor Willis" is having the time of his life! Perhaps you'd better rescue Ben.

Carole exits

Harold Did you pop up for a quarrel or was there something more urgent.

Diane Why? Keeping you from the crossword, am I?

Harold I just wanted ten minutes' peace and quiet, is that so strange?

Diane Words fail me, you don't just pop up to do a crossword puzzle in the middle of a party, even for you it's bizarre, to say the least. . . . You have been in a funny mood all day, why don't

you just come out with whatever is bothering you and let's put
an end to all these childish games.

Harold I have not been in "a very funny mood" or any other kind
of mood to date, but I assure you I shall be in a very bad mood if
you all keep following me around and asking me what's wrong!
I just want to be left alone . . . OK?

Diane All right, Greta Garbo.

Diane exits

Harold returns with a sigh to his paper

After a moment, there is a tap on the door, a pause, then a second tap

Harold (*shouting*) GO AWAY.

*There is another knock and Bess Johnson enters. She is in her late
twenties and very beautiful, with a voluptuous figure shown to
advantage in what appears to be a long cardigan which barely
covers her thighs*

Bess Harold? (*She comes across the room with an exaggerated tip-
toe*) I've been searching for you everywhere.

Harold (*putting down the paper with a sigh*) Really? You were last
reported as being wrapped around my daughter's boyfriend.

Bess (*giggling*) I was trying to put everyone off the scent!

Harold You shouldn't have come here.

Bess (*pouting*) Your wife invited us.

Harold Well she didn't consult me first.

Bess I wanted to see you in your home surroundings.

Harold I think it in very poor taste for you to come at all, after all
this is supposed to be my silver-wedding party!

Bess Well honestly! Isn't that typical of a man! I suppose it's not
in bad taste for you to be having an affair if you're so happily
married?

Harold I didn't say I was happily married, I said it was in poor
taste for you to come to your lover's silver-wedding party.

Bess moves to Harold and sits on his knees

Bess Crosspatch! It was very clever of you to find somewhere we
could be alone together!

Harold I did no such thing! I am supposed to be hiding.

Bess (*pouting*) From me? (*She starts playing with Harold's tie*)

Harold From the combination of you and Diane, she's got a nose like a bloodhound for this sort of thing.

Bess (*freezing on this last remark*) What sort of thing?

Harold (*hastily*) Spotting women she thinks I'd fancy ... (*Changing subject*) What is this ... a cardigan? (*He runs his finger from her throat down over her breasts to her knees*)

Bess (*giggling*) Silly, it's a mini-dress.

Harold It's very nice. (*He kisses her*)

Voices, off

Harold pushes Bess off his lap, knocking over the coffee table in the process. As Bess sprawls on the floor ...

Ben, her husband, enters. He is in his late twenties, and best described as a chinless wonder

Ben Ah there you are, darling. I've been looking everywhere for you. ... What are you doing on the floor, old thing, party games, is it?

Bess I fell over the coffee table.

Ben Oh! Jolly clumsy of you, sweetie. How did you manage that? I mean it's big enough to notice! (*He picks up the table and replaces it*)

Bess What about me?

Ben Oh, sorry darling, should have asked, did you hurt yourself?

Bess (*through gritted teeth*) I mean what about helping me up.

Ben Whoops ... not on the ball tonight ... too many glasses of the old plonk! (*He helps her to her feet*) Wondered where you'd got too, Harold! (*He looks around*) Jolly nice place you've got here.

Harold Thank you.

Bess Are you following me around?

Ben Absolutely not, just wondered where you were.

Bess (*brushing down her dress and trying to straighten her hair*) Why?

Ben Sorry?

Bess Why were you wondering where I was?

Ben (*blankly*) Couldn't find you anywhere.

Bess In other words you are following me around. You know I hate being spied on, if you are going to spend all night spying on me I might as well go home now.

She exits slamming the door

Ben (*standing open-mouthed*) Crumbs!

Harold She seems a bit touchy.

Ben (*gloomily*) Hates to be followed around, should have known better really.

Harold (*curiously*) I've often wondered . . . how did you two meet.

Ben Who?

Harold (*patiently*) You and young Bess. Want a drink?

Ben Oh . . . cheers.

Harold When I want to escape from the woman in my life, I come and hide up here . . . rotten hiding place though, they always find me! (*He hands the can to Ben*) Sorry you'll have to drink it from the can, I only brought one glass.

Ben Quite all right . . .

Harold You were going to tell me where you met young Bess.

Ben We met at university actually.

Harold (*amazed*) You mean Bess went to university?

Ben Oh rather! (*He takes a swig from the can and chokes*)

Harold You amaze me!

Ben Worked as a sort of chambermaid.

Harold Oh I see.

Ben She wanted the experience so she could get a job as an air hostess.

Harold Do they have beds on aeroplanes? Surely not!

Ben No, no, not the bedmaking experiences, the waitress experiences . . . glorified sort of waitresses, aren't they . . . air hostesses?

Harold Well, I think there's a bit more to it than that. So Bess worked as a waitress and a chambermaid, well that's very commendable. Sort of moonlighting as a chambermaid, was she?

Ben (*doubtfully, not having the least idea what Harold is talking about*) Mmm . . . she had the sack, you see, as a waitress, so she got this job as a chambermaid. All the chaps fell for her . . . well, beautiful girl, isn't she? Jolly thrilled when she went out with me I can tell you!

Harold Then you proposed and she accepted and there you are.

Ben Rather! (*He pauses*) I think she's a bit cross . . . hates to be followed, you know.

Harold (*wearily*) Yes, I know.

Diane enters

Diane Would you like us to bring the party up here, Harold?
Ben (*gazing around*) Not much room, not for everyone!
Diane I seem to be celebrating my anniversary on my own.
Harold You exaggerate, I'm just taking a short break from all the excitement.
Diane Carole arranged a surprise cake for us, I can hardly cut it on my own, can I? Would it be too much to ask for you to come downstairs for long enough to cut the cake and maybe pose for a few photos?
Ben (*embarrassed*) I'll be pushing off then, better look for my wife. (*He thinks about it*) On the other hand maybe better not ...

Ben exits

Diane That man is a half-wit.
Harold He's also the boss's son, why does he need brains!
Diane (*sitting on the bed*) Why are you behaving like this?
Harold Like what?
Diane As though all our guests are unwelcome. As though you're leaving me tomorrow.... You know exactly what I mean.

Harold gets up and wanders round the room

Harold I have a headache ...
Diane Good Lord, I thought only women made that excuse ...! Shall I put you out of your misery? If it's because I've invited your current mistress here, there's really no need to be embarrassed. After all if I were to leave out all the women of our acquaintance you have slept with or made passes at, there would be hardly anyone left to invite, would there?
Harold (*totally dumbfounded*) Come again?
Diane I realize the current one is a bit awkward ...
Harold Hold on ... what are you talking about?
Diane I'm trying to tell you that all this skulking about is quite unnecessary, that's all.
Harold Have you gone potty?
Diane I mean there's no need to hide, I'm not bothered.
Harold You don't give a damn is what you really mean.
Diane I'm a realist ... you really haven't covered your tracks all

that well over the years you know! I have always known about your little romances, in fact I could probably tell you when each affair began and when it ended. I got to read the signs after a while. . . . Most of the time you were pretty obvious . . . of course I minded a great deal in the early days . . . I thought it was all my fault . . . that I'd failed you in some way, then I started to see it as it really was. The truth is, you were always a randy sod and one woman was never going to be enough. I knew you loved me, well, as much as you were capable of loving. I settled for that. You always came home in the end . . . I happen to think that adultery is not a good enough reason for breaking up a marriage . . . not if all the other things are there. I think it's worth a row or a fur coat but divorce for adultery's sake . . .

Harold (*blankly*) Worth a fur coat?

Diane Yes . . . by way of showing you're sorry, if the marriage is good otherwise, if it works, our marriage works in most respects. . . . I must admit I didn't realize you were currently involved with Ben's wife . . . but I was aware you were on the toot again . . . so to speak.

Harold Whoa . . . hold on a minute . . . have you ever stopped to ask why I should need affection from other women? Not that I'm admitting this is anything but utter rubbish, but supposing it to be true, shouldn't you be asking yourself why?

Diane Oh don't lay that one on me, Harold, not the neglected husband routine . . . spare me that!

Harold I think if you were honest you'd agree that you haven't been that interested in sex. I concede I flirt a bit. Maybe sometimes things have gone a bit further than they should . . . when I've had a bit too much to drink . . . I'm no saint . . . but if a woman is cold towards you . . .

Diane (*standing up*) You have this knack of never being at fault whatever the circumstances, there's always someone else to blame. In all the years I've known you I can never remember hearing you say you were in the wrong . . . it's a rare talent, you should have gone into politics . . . your mother didn't have an affair with a Russian by any chance, did she?

Harold You're taking this very calmly I must say . . . then you've always been an unfeeling woman . . .

Diane (*calmly*) We are supposed to be cutting the cake.

Harold (*now thoroughly incensed*) Oh fine, you tell me what a bastard I am and then we go and blow the candles out on our wedding-cake ... you are a heartless bitch ... if you wanted to wash all our dirty linen in public couldn't it have waited until after the party?

Diane I thought you weren't admitting anything, aren't you a little confused? You're unbelievable, do you know that? I should have known this would turn out to be all my fault! You spend our anniversary hiding in the bedroom because I have inadvertently invited your current mistress to our party, and then when I finally fall in and realize what the problem is and tell you, that far from it being a well-kept secret, I have known for years that you can't keep your hands off anything in skirts ... suddenly, I am the heartless bitch who has ruined your life. You amaze me, you really do! What's more I am not washing our dirty linen in public, there's no-one here but us ... unless blondie is hiding under the bed.

Harold Nobody is under the bed ... still as you seem to have doubted my every word for the last twenty-five years perhaps you'd better check!

Diane I'm not interested enough to look.

Harold Well you should be ... what kind of woman are you anyway, why aren't you scratching her eyes out if you think I'm having an affair ... it's not normal for a woman to say "I know I made a boo-boo and invited your mistress to our anniversary party but let's cut the cake and forget it". No wonder I'm confused—any self-respecting man would be confused!

Diane I'm glad you respect yourself ... I can't say I respect you. I'd respect you more if you behaved a bit more like a man and less like a sulky schoolboy. You're pathetic—I feel like your mother half the time.... Do you know it took me less than an hour to work out why you were hiding tonight.... "What has he been up too" I pondered, a quick elimination of the suspects and bingo!

Harold In other words you jumped to conclusions!

Diane Conclusions based on years of experience.

Harold No proof though!

Diane If I'd wanted proof I'm sure I'd have found it without too much effort, you haven't exactly covered your tracks, have you? It's like I told you, you've been a good provider, a good father— even a good husband in a strange way.... Why rock the boat?

Harold Where does love come in? Where is the jealousy, the passion.... How can you calmly stand there and say in effect that it doesn't matter what I do as long as I bring home the money, clean the windows and cut the grass.

The door opens and Carole comes in carrying a wine bottle

Carole Dad! I ... Oh hello, Mum ... (*She tries to hide the bottle*) I just thought I'd come and see if Dad was feeling OK.

Harold gets up and removes the bottle from Carole

Harold I am feeling absolutely marvellous.... Why don't you compare notes on what could possibly be wrong with me.

Harold exits

Carole Dad? (*She makes a move to follow Harold*)
Diane (*wearily*) Oh, let him go. (*She sinks on to the bed*)
Carole What's the matter with him?
Diane I think I've hurt his pride.... Silly, isn't it? I've kept my mouth shut for twenty-five years and blown it on what should be a celebration of our lives together, we've made it! Isn't that what tonight is supposed to say? Other marriages might fall down but ours has stayed the distance ... what a farce.
Carole I don't know what you're talking about.
Diane I don't suppose you do ... (*She moves to the dressing table and sits staring into the mirror*) Where should I begin? On our wedding-day, perhaps, when he spent half the night chatting up the prettiest guests—or maybe it was later than that. The first time I knew he was seriously involved with another woman I wanted to die—up till then I just told myself he liked to flirt. Then I got this anonymous letter ... I was going to show him but he was very late home that night. I had time to think, decide what I was going to say, you know how you hold conversations in your mind? What you'll say, what they'll reply—only in my mind.... The answers were all coming out wrong. I was precipitating some sort of crisis ... her or me? I tore the letter up and when he came home I said nothing. I started noticing things of course but I kept silent. I knew when it ended—and when the next one began. I was watching out for the signs, oh, I was on the alert all right. I wouldn't be fooled again, no sir, not me ... I knew when each one began, and ended. After a bit none of them

hurt anymore ... not much anyway, I knew he loved me. I knew he would never leave us.... You and I—we were reality, the rest were romance, ego boosting. After a bit I stopped looking for signs. It all seemed a bit silly.... That girl—Ben's wife—I had no idea, then when he started acting like a spoilt child tonight, I suddenly realized—he was embarrassed. I'd invited his latest mistress to our home on our silver wedding.... Bad form, wasn't it? Past mistresses are all right but present mistresses.... Well, it's not quite the thing. (*She takes off her ear-rings and throws them into the jewellery box*)

Carole crosses over and kneels beside her

Carole Oh Mum!
Diane I told him I knew! Why oh why did I tell him? I've kept quiet so long ... why did I tell him now?
Carole I always thought you didn't know.
Diane You mean you knew? (*She turns and stares at her*)
Carole Oh yes, I mean, well everyone knows, don't they? He's a bit of a joke really. Well I don't mean that exactly, he's more of a naughty schoolboy. It's never stopped me loving him. Funny I don't think I was ever even shocked about it, Dad and his flirtations, I just presumed you were the one person who didn't know ... I couldn't have put up with it in a husband, in someone else it's disgusting ... but in Dad it seemed ... well, Dad ... Dad the lady-killer, a joke, as long as you weren't hurt ... well it's ... Dad, isn't it.
Diane You do realize it was often a bit more than flirting!
Carole Yes of course I do.... Well I do now, since I grew up I mean.
Diane You shock me, Carole, you really do ... if my father had played around ... I don't think I could have forgiven him.
Carole Well times have changed, haven't they? I mean everyone's at it these days.
Diane I'm not.
Carole Perhaps that's where you've gone wrong, maybe you should have played him at his game.
Diane (*simply*) I never wanted anyone else.
Carole Well I shouldn't worry too much, let's face it, his pulling days have got to be numbered.
Diane You really haven't understood, have you? The only reason

this marriage has survived is because I always kept my head, pretended I didn't know ... and the reason I did that was because I knew it wasn't important ... we were important.

Carole Of course I've understood ... you said that before.

Diane (*shouting*) But I've told him I know ... that I've always known.... His pride won't be able to deal with that ... things will never be the same again.

Carole Maybe they'll be better. It seems to me that for the last couple of generations, fidelity has gone out of the window. Well, maybe I'm old-fashioned but for me that's a shame. I want a man who only wants me. I won't settle for less. I agree, if you have the misfortune to be married to a womanizer you have two choices ... walk away or turn a blind eye. Well, obviously your decision was to turn a blind eye ... personally I couldn't have done that, I wouldn't have been able to live with it. I love him, he's been a terrific father—a lousy husband but as a father— faultless, and I think you are partly to blame for his shortcomings as a husband. He got away with what you allowed him to get away with.... Well now the worm has turned, big deal ... what do you imagine is going to happen? I agree his pride will be hurt ... but so what? He isn't going to leave you—let's face it—who else would put up with him?

Diane (*blowing her nose loudly*) Oh Carole.

Carole So powder your nose and get back down there and cut your cake.

Diane Do me one favour, ask him to come back up here and speak to me, if he's not run away that is.

Carole Not him, stuck down a bottle of scotch more like.

Carole kisses Diane on the top of her head and exits

Diane makes an effort to tidy her hair and put on some lipstick. As she does so ...

The door opens and Ben enters

Ben Sorry. (*He stands hesitantly in the doorway*) I was just looking for my wife.

Diane (*turning to look at him*) Have you lost her?

Ben I seem to have upset her ... she might have gone home ... thought I was following her around you see.

Diane Were you?

Ben (*shocked*) Lord no, wouldn't do that, drives her mad, wouldn't upset her for the world . . .

Diane Why did she think you were following her around?

Ben (*rubbing his ear and looking vague*) Came into the room and she flew into a temper . . . just wondered if she was all right . . . might have been ill . . . wasn't following her you see . . . just looking for her . . . not the same thing at all.

Diane No of course it's not. (*She hesitates*) Was she on her own?

Ben (*surprised*) No, not on her own, I came with her, you invited us.

Diane No I didn't mean to the party, I meant did she . . . was she . . . was she in the room on her own, when you came to look for her?

Ben No, Harold was with her . . . on the floor.

Diane Harold was on the floor with her!

Ben No no. She was on the floor. Harold was on the settee.

Diane What was she doing on the floor?

Ben Fell over.

Diane Really, how did she manage to do that?

Ben Didn't ask . . . got annoyed . . . said I was following her about . . . went off in a huff.

Diane I see . . . (*She gets up and moves downstage*) Ben, come and sit down a minute. (*She gestures to the chaise-longue*)

Ben comes over and sits perched on the edge of the chaise-longue, looking uncomfortable

Ben, I want to have a serious talk to you.

Ben looks alarmed

I am old enough to be your mother, so I am going to talk to you like a mother, all right?

Ben Oh no, Mother's a lot older, much younger than Mother . . . prettier too.

Diane (*gratified*) Thank you, Ben, nevertheless I am going to pretend I'm your mother.

Ben Oh charades, is it?

Diane No, Ben, not charades, serious business.

Ben Haven't offended you, have I?

Diane Now how would you have offended me?

Ben Don't know, always putting my foot in it.

Diane Well you haven't offended me, this is about Bess.
Ben Ah.
Diane About you and Bess.
Ben Following her about you mean, shouldn't do it, right?
Diane No, no that's not it. . . . Oh dear this is so difficult. How can
I put this . . . Ben, if you bring your wife to a party and she
disappears you have every right to be concerned, every right to
come and look for her, that is courteous, you are a courteous
person, Bess has no right to be angry with you for that. You
must stick up for yourself, be firm.
Ben Oh no, dash it all . . . very pretty girl . . . wouldn't want to
upset her.
Diane She is a very pretty girl but she is also a very lucky girl,
lucky because she has a very nice husband who cares about her
feelings . . . this is really not for me to say but . . . well I like you
very much and it concerns me that if you treat Bess too gently
she will despise you for it, women don't admire men who let
them get away with too much, you know?
Ben Not the sort of chap to go round making scenes.
Diane Of course you're not, I didn't mean you should make
scenes, just be a bit firm.
Ben A bit firm.
Diane Yes, let me give you an example. (*She gazes around for
inspiration*) Get on the floor.
Ben On the floor?
Diane Yes, get on the floor, pretend you're Bess and I'll show you
what I mean.
Ben (*light dawning*) Oh, like this. (*He lies on the floor, has an
afterthought, gets up and turns over the coffee table*)
Diane What did you do that for?
Ben Coffee table was on the floor too.
Diane Was it indeed . . . all right Ben, now I'll be you coming in.
Ben Should have Harold here really.
Diane (*grimly*) We'll imagine Harold, shall we.
Ben Right-o.
Diane OK. . . . "What the hell are you doing down there?"
Ben (*scrambling to his feet*) You told me to get down there!
Diane No, no, get back down again, I was being you then.
Ben Oh sorry. (*He lies down again*)
Diane Right now, I am pretending to be you and I've come in and

found you lying on the floor. . . . "What the hell are you doing down there?"

Silence

Well go on then, you be Bess.
Ben Right-o.

A pause

Diane Well.
Ben What?
Diane Lord give me patience. . . . What would Bess say?
Ben I think she'd wonder what I was doing on the floor, don't know what she'd say though.
Diane (*patiently*) What would Bess have said if you had come into the room and asked her what the hell was going on.
Ben Oh, of course, sorry . . . she'd probably say something like "Who do you think you're shouting at?"
Diane That's the idea. . . . "Never mind changing the subject I asked you what you were doing on the floor."
Ben I say this is good fun, isn't it . . .

Diane glares at him

(*Improvising hastily*) "I fell over."
Diane "Really . . . fell over what?"
Ben Ah, asked her that . . . (*He thinks*) Said she fell over the coffee table.
Diane (*icily*) "You expect me to believe that!"
Ben No truly, that's what she said, said she fell over the coffee table.
Diane (*trying to be patient*) When I said "Do you expect me to believe that" I was pretending to be you. . . . That's what you should have replied.
Ben Right-o. (*He pauses until he catches Diane's eye and then he hastily enters back into the spirit of things. In a high falsetto voice*) "How dare you!"
Diane Good . . . "I don't believe you. I Think there's something going on. . . . Get your coat I'm taking you home!"
Ben (*shocked*) Couldn't have said that! Not to Bess! Wouldn't have gone anyway, waste of time suggesting it.
Diane That's the point I'm trying to make, Ben, if you were more

... well, masterful ... she would have gone home with you. You see if you spoke firmly to her she would have admired you. Women, even strong-minded women like me, well we like to feel a man is the boss, stronger. When it comes right down to it we want to be bossed. If a man lets us get away with too much, well ... we despise him.

Ben (*doubtfully*) Really?

Diane (*firmly*) Absolutely.

Ben Right-o.

Diane You should start being firm with Bess, I think you'll find she likes it.... Once she gets over the shock, that is.

Ben (*after a long pause*) Know I'm a bit slow on the old uptake, used to call me Bertie Wooster at Oxford but—well—are you saying there was something going on? I mean—dash it all—Harold is your husband ... he's my friend ... I mean this is your anniversary ... you don't mean ...

Diane (*helping him out*) I think Harold is a dreadful flirt and Bess is a very pretty girl.... If I were a man and I walked into a room and found my wife alone with a man and sprawled on the floor ... well I think I would have asked a few questions.

Ben (*shaken*) Oh.

Diane gets down on the floor next to Ben and takes his hand

Diane I'm not suggesting anything, so don't go upsetting yourself, I just think you should have asked a few pertinent questions.

The door opens and Bess enters; she has obviously had a great deal to drink and stands swaying in the doorway for a few minutes

Bess Peepboo! Still hiding, are we? Still sulking.... Where are you? (*She spots Diane and Ben*) Hello hello hello, what have we here ... wifey lying down next to Bensy.

Both Diane and Ben scramble to their feet

Ben It's not what it looks like, sweetie.

Bess I know it's not what it looks like, sugar plum, anyone but you and I would have had serious doubts, but knowing how seriously undersexed you are I fully believe there is some simple explanation. (*She sways and sits down abruptly on the bed*)

Diane (*incensed*) You cow!

Bess (*giggling*) Ooh dear, I've upset wifey ... so sorry. (*She* *hiccups*) I didn't mean you were seriously undersexed ... I meant Bensy there! (*She waves vaguely*) I'm sure you're a wow in the sack.

Diane (*dangerously*) Did my husband tell you that? I must say I'm surprised ... I always imagined straying husbands told a different tale, a sort of variation on the "Wife doesn't understand me" theme, more like "Of course that side of things has been over for years, she never was very interested and now we live like brother and sister". Isn't that how the story goes?

Bess (*struggling to keep her wits about her*) How should I know?

Diane I thought you were an expert on married men, I mean I can't believe Harold is the first.

Ben (*confused*) I say hang on a minute.

Diane I'll tell you one thing though, he deserves a lot better than you!

Bess Harold?

Diane No, Ben. . . . God knows what a gentle sweet person like him saw in an old slag like you.

Bess tries to get off the bed and falls back down again. Diane crosses over and stands in front of her whilst Ben vainly tries to pull her away

Ben I say—you mustn't say things like that ...

Diane (*warming to her theme*) And I'll tell you another thing, if you think you're different in some way let me disillusion you. . . . You are merely the latest in the long line of women with whom my husband has amused himself and I have no doubts that you will go the same way as the others. . . . I'm sure you follow me!

Bess (*stumbling over her words*) I'm sure I don't know what you mean. If you are suggesting I am involved with your husband—I do not need your husband. (*She hiccups*) I have a perfectly good husband of my own. If you can't hang on to a man that's your lookout. I think if a man has to carry on with other women you need to look to yourself. I should think you must be lacking in something ... who knows. Anyway, why pick on me? I wasn't the one rolling around on the carpet with someone else's husband ... I'm the one with an axe to grind.

Ben (*impressed*) That's true you know!

Diane (*turning on him*) Oh don't be a bloody fool, she was on the floor earlier, you told me so yourself.

Bess (*getting to her feet, waving her arms around*) Well that's very

nice I must say. So you've been discussing me with all and
sundry, have you. Well I must say I think—— (*She flops back on
the bed and passes out*)
Ben (*anguished*) Bess ... Bess ...
Diane Oh take no notice she's only doing it for effect. (*She bends
over and peers at Bess*) Good grief she's paralytic, however has
she got in this state?
Ben She doesn't drink much.
Diane I'm glad to hear she doesn't do everything to excess!
Ben (*puzzled*) What?
Diane Never mind, look she can't stay here all night, you're going
to have to get her home somehow. . . . God, this evening really is
turning into an anniversary to remember!

She shakes Bess who grunts and rolls over

I refuse to put her up for the night, can you get her out of here?
Ben (*helpfully*) Got the car downstairs.
Diane I doubt you'd be able to carry her to the car ... (*She thinks*)
I'll try and get someone to help you ... (*She moves towards the
door then stops and thinks a second or two*) On second thoughts
I'll help you myself ... I think we've given the relatives enough
to talk about for one evening ... (*She opens the door and looks
out*) No-one about ... (*She crosses to the bed*) Can you manage
a fireman's lift?
Ben Rather! (*He pauses*) Carry her out and put her in the car you
mean?
Diane That was the idea yes.
Ben Right-o.

*They both struggle and between them manage to put Bess over Ben's
shoulder*

Diane Right, I'll open the door and you take her downstairs ... if
anyone comes out just make a joke, you know, say she's passed
out and you're taking her home.
Ben (*puzzled*) Aren't I taking her home?
Diane Of course you are.
Ben (*mystified*) Right.

Ben moves towards the door and Diane opens it

Harold enters

Harold What the hell . . .
Ben Taking her home . . . had too much to drink!
Harold (*ignoring him*) What's been going on!
Diane I knocked her out.
Harold What!
Diane (*impatiently*) She's passed out for God's sake—not before
 we told each other a few home truths I'm glad to say!
Ben (*panting*) Shall I put her down?
Diane (*holding the door open*) No, just take her away.

Ben exits then almost immediately returns

Ben Sorry, forgot my manners, lovely party.

Ben shakes hands with Harold who looks blankly at him

 (*To Diane*) Jolly nice party, thanks again.
Diane Good-night Ben.

Ben exits

Harold What do you mean you told each other a few home truths?
Diane I called her a slag and she called me a sexless cow who
 couldn't keep a man, or words to that effect.
Harold Oh fantastic—whilst Ben stood by agog no doubt.
Diane I think most of it was over Ben's head.
Harold I suppose you did pause to remember his father just
 happens to be my employer, not to mention the fact that Ben is
 not quite as stupid as he looks.
Diane Well he couldn't be, could he?
Harold You might have just ruined my career, I hope that thought
 gives you some satisfaction.
Diane You've ruined my life . . . it seems a fair exchange!
Harold I haven't changed, Diane, I am the same man you married.
Diane True. You are the same cheating bastard you always were.
Harold Everyone seems to be leaving, that's what I came up to tell
 you.
Diane Well that's hardly surprising, is it? Thanks for a super
 wedding anniversary.
Harold Don't mention it.

As they glare at each other . . .

 The door opens and Carole enters crying

Carole Mum ... Dad. (*She falls on to Harold's chest sobbing loudly*)
Harold Darling ...?
Diane Sweetheart, what's happened?
Carole Oh Mum, it's awful. (*She sobs some more*)

Harold and Diane cuddle Carole and together they take her down to the chaise-longue and sit her down

Harold Just tell us, baby ... (*He hands her a hanky*)
Carole (*sobbing*) It's Willis ...
Diane What's happened?
Harold If he's been interfering with you in some way ...
Carole Oh Daddy, don't be stupid.
Diane Just tell us, darling, you can tell us anything you know that.
Carole He's been dancing all night with that little tart of a wife of Ben's and I've just found him in the garden being sick ... and, oh Daddy ...
Diane What, what?
Harold Yes, what?
Carole (*wailing*) He admitted he'd made love to her in the greenhouse.
Harold (*stupified*) My greenhouse!
Diane Your greenhouse, your mistress, seems fair.
Harold (*jumping up*) The filthy little swine.
Diane Oh don't be ridiculous, the woman's a man-eater.
Carole I don't care whose fault it is. (*She bursts into sobs again*) How could he.
Diane Well if he was drunk ...
Harold What kind of excuse is that?
Diane You tell me! I always thought drunk meant incapable!
Harold You're well rid of him.
Carole I don't want to be rid of him—I love him.
Harold Well you've finished with him I can assure you. What kind of future could you have with a man who behaves like that behind your back.
Diane If you can spare an hour or two I'll give you a quick synopsis ...
Harold This is not the time for sarcasm, Diane ... Can't you see how distressed the child is?
Carole At least he was honest about it. I think she threw herself at

him. Anyone can see what kind of a woman she is ... a few drinks and she's anyone's.

Diane Well some people would certainly be able to spot that at a glance I agree.

Carole My own father's mistress ... (*She bursts into loud sobs again*)

Harold (*stunned*) What did you say? (*He rounds on Diane*) What have you been saying to her?

Diane Nothing she didn't already know.

Harold I wouldn't have believed even you would stoop so low.

Diane Well you've got a nerve.

Carole Stop it both of you.... My life is ruined and all you can do is squabble with each other ... I thought you'd understand.... Oh I wish I was dead! (*She buries her face in the settee*)

Diane Hush, darling ... of course we understand.

Harold You only think your heart is broken but honestly, darling, any man who behaves like that.... You've had a lucky escape believe me.

Carole I don't want to escape, why don't you listen? I keep telling you ... I want it not to have happened, and I want to kill him ... and her.

Diane (*soothingly*) Of course you do, my poor darling, never mind, it will all seem much better in the morning, after a good night's sleep.

Harold Don't be fatuous, Diane, how will it seem better in the morning for God's sake, can't you see the child is overwrought?

Diane Things always seem better in the daytime—I don't know why—they just do.

Harold If you're totally insensitive they might ... some people do not recover from a broken heart by taking a quick trip round Harrods with an American Express card.

Diane I just mean it won't seem so dreadful in the cold light of day. The boy obviously had too much to drink and some cheap little tart has thrown herself at him.... It happens all the time.

Carole He said he loved me.... How could he?

Diane A standing prick hath no conscience ...

Harold Well that's a charming expression to use in front of your only daughter.

Diane I learnt it at my mother's knee.

Harold That I can believe. Your mother's got a lot to answer for.

Diane What exactly is that supposed to mean?

Harold I mean her well-known hatred of the male sex has doubt-less led to your being the woman you are today.

Carole (*sitting up and blowing her nose*) Please! I don't want to listen to this. I don't need it, just forget it, I don't want to talk about it anymore, not tonight, I'm going to bed.

Harold Shall I——

Carole Just let me sleep on it, Daddy, all right?

Diane Would you like me to——

Carole I'd just like to be left alone. (*She gets up and blows her nose again*) Good-night.

Carole exits

Harold (*reluctantly*) Good-night . . . (*He watches her exit and then turns to Diane*) Well you were a big help . . . spouting platitudes, I stand by what I said, she's well rid of him . . . drunk indeed! As for you filling her head with all this rubbish about the woman being my mistress! Pure fantasy! The whole thing's disgusting! In my greenhouse too! The man's an animal. . . . What are you smiling at!

Diane You.

Harold (*offended*) I think I've behaved with admirable restraint. If I'd said what I really thought! Fifty years ago I'd have seen to it he was horsewhipped!

Diane She loves him.

Harold Don't be ridiculous, she can do a great deal better than that oaf.

Diane I don't happen to think you can do better than a man you love, I rather thought I was living proof.

Harold I hope you're not suggesting there's any similarity between his behaviour and mine? Anyway, it's quite different with us.

Diane Why is that?

Harold You and Carole come first in my life, always will.

Diane Do you think I don't know that? It's why I'm still here.

Harold Don't start that again. I don't think I'm so hard to live with . . . (*He looks at her wistfully*) Am I?

Diane Most of the time, no.

Harold Well then. (*He undoes his tie*)

Diane I've learnt to live with your flaws, no use trying to change you now, I suppose.

Harold (*dignified*) I admit to no flaws.

Diane (*crossing to the dressing table*) Well that's in character at least.

Harold (*complacently*) I think I know you well enough, to be pretty sure that if you really thought I'd been having affairs all over the place you'd have never been able to keep your mouth shut, you'd have kicked me out years ago. . . . You just talk for effect.

Diane sits at the table and starts to remove her make-up

Diane You could be right.

Harold Take tonight, just because I wasn't in a party mood you have to fantasize.

Diane Is that what I do?

Harold (*cunningly*) I put it down to the menopause, when you get in these moods you just put two and two together and make eight, don't you?

Diane Something like that.

Harold You've always been a very dramatic woman. (*He starts taking off his shoes and socks*) Tomorrow you'd better have a serious talk to that girl . . . or I will.

Diane You'll be too busy.

Harold Doing what?

Diane Tomorrow you're going out to buy me an extra special anniversary present.

Harold (*indignant*) I've already bought you a present! That watch cost me an arm and a leg!

Diane (*still removing her make-up*) It's lovely but . . .

Harold But what?

Diane Well . . . what I'd really like . . . what I've always wanted . . . is a fur coat.

Harold pauses, turns and looks at her as——

—the CURTAIN *falls*

FURNITURE AND PROPERTY LIST

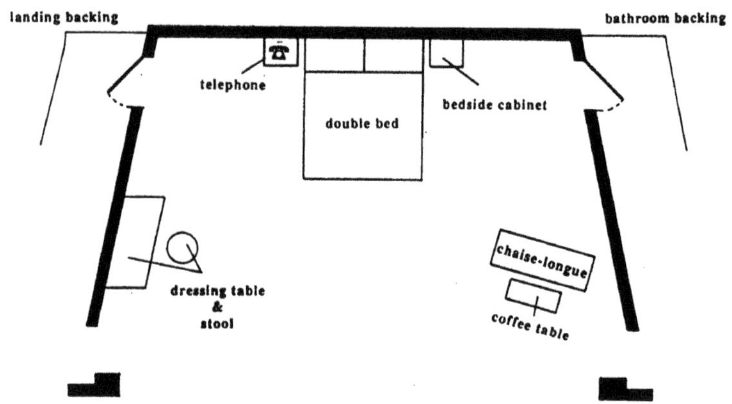

SCENE 1

On stage: Double bed. *On it:* **Harold**'s shirt and jacket
2 bedside cabinets. *On one of them:* telephone. *In drawer:* jewel
box containing ear-rings
Dressing table. *On it:* toilet items, glass of gin and tonic
Stool
Chaise-longue
Coffee table

Off stage: Nil

Personal: **Harold:** wrist-watch (required throughout)

SCENE 2

On stage: As end of Scene 1

Off stage: Glass, 2 cans of lager, newspaper **(Harold)**
Wine bottle **(Carole)**

Personal: **Harold:** pen, handkerchief

LIGHTING PLOT

Property fittings required: *nil*

Interior. The same scene throughout

SCENE 1

To open: General interior lighting

Cue 1   **Harold** exits   (Page 4)
           Black-out

SCENE 2

To open: General interior lighting

No cues

EFFECTS PLOT

No cues

MADE AND PRINTED IN GREAT BRITAIN BY
LATIMER TREND & COMPANY LTD PLYMOUTH

MADE IN ENGLAND